10
Out of this
World Jokes

by Morgan Matthews

Watermill Press

Library of Congress Cataloging-in-Publication Data

Matthews, Morgan.
    102 out of this world jokes / by Morgan Matthews.
      p.   cm.
    Summary: A collection of 102 riddle jokes about outer space,
including ''Why did the moon refuse to eat lunch? Because it was
full.''
    ISBN 0-8167-2789-9 (pbk.)
    1. Wit and humor, Juvenile. 2. Outer space—Juvenile humor.
[1. Outer space—Wit and humor. 2. Riddles. 3. Jokes.] I. Title.
II. Title: One hundred two out of this world jokes.
PN6163.M277 1992
818'.5402—dc20   91-45021

What did the alien gas man say to the earthling?

"Take me to your meter."

What kind of music do aliens like?

Moon rock.

What is the best way to wash a dirty meteor?

Put it in a meteor shower.

What does an asteroid use to hold up its pants?

An asteroid belt.

How can you tell how old Saturn is?

Count its rings.

Who was the first deer in space?

Buck Rogers.

What do you get if you cross an android with a skunk?

R2-PU.

What does a Martian write notes on while blasting into space?

A launching pad.

Why did the alien come to Earth and climb a tree?

He wanted to have a close encounter of the bird kind.

What's the best way to clean meteors?

Use Comet® cleanser.

Why did the nuclear-powered android go to the doctor?

He had atomic ache.

Why did the Martian lawyer go to court?

He had to settle a space suit.

What did the hip satellite say to the moon rocker?

"You put me in orbit."

What did Mr. Spock say when Kirk called him?

"I'm all ears, Captain."

When do the planets celebrate?

When a star is born.

Which radio channel do Martians listen to?

The space station.

What do you call a magician from Mars?

An unidentified flying sorcerer.

What's out in space and goes ka-pow! ka-pow?

A shooting star.

KA-pow!

KA-pow!

Which planet has a laundry problem?

Saturn. It has ring around the collar.

Where do you put a scoop of space ice cream?

In a nose cone.

What do you call an alien skunk?

A space scenter.

What does a Martian astronaut keep snacks in?

A launch bag.

Why did the man from Mars go to a tailor?

He wanted to have a clothes encounter.

How do you find a lost star?

Follow its star tracks.

What kind of plants grow in space?

Alien beans (beings).

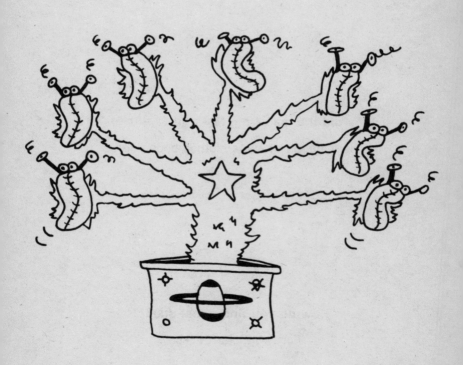

What do you call a space taxi that can't find a job?

An unemployed flying object.

What has less calories than a full moon?

Moon Lite.

Who fought in Star Wars and oinks?

Ham Solo.

What sound does an alarm clock make on the moon?

Lunaticks.

Which candy do Martians like to eat?

Milky Way® bars.

What should you do for a depressed rocket?

Boost its confidence.

What do Martian football players wear?

Space helmets.

What do men from space drink?

E-Tea.

Why is traveling into space so much fun?

It's a blast right from the start.

Why don't space robots make good musicians?

They all have tin ears.

Why don't stars have to exercise?

They have heavenly bodies.

Why were the alien newlyweds so happy?

They were on a honey*moon*.

What do you call a bunch of alien cub scouts?

The den from Mars.

How did the nose cone get soggy?

From rocket tears (rocketeers).

Which T.V. show did the alien magician star in?

Star Trick.

What do Martian families do after dinner?

They wash the satellite dishes.

What's found in space and has an agent?

A movie star.

What do you call moon music?

Luna Tunes.

How do you stop a baby flying saucer from crying?

Rock it.

What's another name for the cluster of stars known as Pisces?

Starfish.

Why did the alien squirrel come to Earth?

He was looking for astro*nuts*.

What did the spaceman name his gun?

Ray.

What do you call dull aliens?

Star Bores.

How do you catch a space fish?

Use a pla*net*.

What has wheels, carries 8 passengers, and flies?

A space station wagon.

What does a U.F.O. wear under its dress?

A star slip.

Why did the Martians put an addition on their house?

They needed more space.

What fish do you find in space?

The Neptuna.

What did the spaceman say to the dog?

Take me to your breeder.

What's greasy and comes from outer space?

A frying saucer.

What happens if a space rocket catches cold?

Its nose cone gets clogged up.

Which planet is very musical?

Nep*tune.*

Where do young Martians go in the summertime?

Space camp.

What do you call a scary alien?

A star frighter.

What do you call a space robot named Elizabeth?

A tin lizzie.

What did Neptune say to Saturn?

Give me a ring sometime.

What do you call a film about bugs in space?

A sci-fly movie.

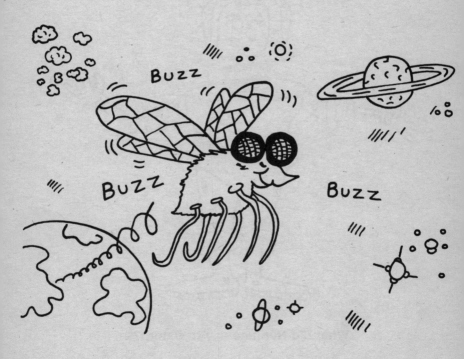

What did the alien tea kettle say to the Scottish space stove?

"Steam me up, Scotty."

Which organization cheers for rockets when they launch?

The Booster Club.

What did one satellite in orbit say to the other?

"I can't go around with you anymore."

What should you do if you see a blue moon?

Try to cheer him up.

Why did the aliens take a maid into outer space?

To star dust.

Which space villain works in a restaurant?

Darth Waiter.

Is Martian food good?

Yes. It tastes out of this world!

Why don't space robots ever get ill?

They have iron stomachs.

**What does a little Martian do when he's afraid to
sleep in a dark space ship?**

He turns on a satellite.

What do you see during halftime at an alien football game?

A Martian band.

What do you find in a lunar playground?

The dark slide of the moon.

What kind of music do alien robots like?

Heavy metal music.

What's the best way to capture a pilot from Venus?

Use a Venus Flytrap.

Who is the hero of Neptune Pond?

Splash Gordon.

What did the meteor say to the earth's atmosphere?

You burn me up!

What did one cool alien say to the other?

Yo! You're a far-out dude!

What would you call an ocean on the moon?

Luna sea.

Why did the plump Martian go into space?

He wanted to be weightless.

What did the android give the robot on Valentine's Day?

A box of chocolate-covered nuts and bolts.

What does a barber do to the moon's hair?

Eclipse it (He clips it).

How did Mars become the red planet?

It stayed out in the sun too long.

How did the meteor get a black eye?

An asteroid belted him.

What do spacemen put in their cocoa?

Martianmallows.

What do you call a Martian werewolf?

An interplanet-hairy monster.

Which planet smells the best?

The sun. It's the scenter of our universe.

Which planet costs 25 cents?

The quarter moon.

Why did Mrs. Martian move to a new galaxy?

She needed her own space.

Why did the moon refuse to eat lunch?

It was full.

What did the rocket say to the astronaut before lift-off?

"Give me a boost up."

Why was the asteroid actor unhappy?

He couldn't get star billing.

What do you call amateur alien artists?

Space crafters.

What flies through space and goes toot! toot?

A space*ship*.

What did Sheriff Gravity say to the outlaw rockets?

"Give up, boys. You can't escape Gravity."

Which reptile flies in UFOs?

The navi*gator*.

What do you call a dumb spaceship?

Rocket Fool.

Where do aliens go to report a crime?

The police space station.

What does the sun do when it's in trouble?

It sends up a solar flare.

What do Martians have at 12 noon?

A space launch.

What do you call a dumb Martian?

A real spacehead.

Why was Saturn so happy?

It just got an engagement ring.